France Gagnon Pratte

The
Banff Springs
HOTEL
The Castle in the Rockies

CANADIAN PACIFIC
HOTELS

ÉDITIONS
CONTINUITE

Canadian Cataloguing in Publication data

Gagnon Pratte, France

    The Banff Springs Hotel

    Includes bibliographical references.

    ISBN 2-9803575-8-8 (pbk.)
    ISBN 2-9803575-9-6 (bound)

    1. Banff Springs Hotel — History. 2. Hotels — Alberta — Banff — History.
3. Architecture — Alberta — Banff. I. Title.

TX941.B35G33 1998   647.947123′32   C98-940003-4

PROJECT DIRECTOR AND AUTHOR:	France Gagnon Pratte
PROJECT COORDINATOR:	Micheline Piché
RESEARCH:	France Gagnon Pratte
COPY-EDITING AND PROOF READING:	Linda Blythe
BOOK DESIGN:	Norman Dupuis
COVER PHOTOGRAPH:	CP Hotel Archives
ELECTRONIC PRE-PRESS:	Compelec inc.
PRINTER:	Imprimerie La Renaissance inc.

©   Éditions Continuité inc.
     82, Grande Allée Ouest, Québec QC G1R 2G6

     France Gagnon Pratte

Produced exclusively for Canadian Pacific Stores Limited

Legal deposit Québec and Ottawa - 3rd Quarter 1997

ISBN 2-9803575-8-8 (soft cover)

ISBN 2-9803575-9-6 (hard cover)

ACKNOWLEDGMENTS

This book is dedicated to my grandchildren, Julien and Béatrix.

There are many individuals whose help and enthusiasm made this book possible, the most important ones being Robert DeMone, President of Canadian Pacific Hotels and Edward Kissane, Regional Vice President and General Manager of the Banff Springs Hotel. The research for the book was done at the Canadian Pacific Archives in Montreal and a special thanks goes to Nancy Williatte-Battet who worked with me providing historical and photographic material that was essential.

It is also important to acknowledge the previous works on the history of the Canadian Pacific Railway which helped me understand the role played by the Banff Springs in the history of Canada. The remarkable books by Pierre Berton on the railway saga, by Walter Vaughan on Sir William Van Horne and other works such as those by E.J. Hart, Harold Kalman and Bart Robinson provided the historical background for this study. In Banff Springs, the contribution of historian Robert Sandford was important as his knowledge of the history of Banff, the CPR relationship with Parks Canada and the development of the mountaineering programs was invaluable. His contribution was greatly appreciated.

Finally, I wish to express gratitude to Linda Blythe for revision and copy-editing, and to Micheline Piché, Director of Les Éditions Continuité.

FRANCE GAGNON PRATTE

TABLE OF CONTENTS

The Banff Springs hotel is the oldest of the heritage railway hotels of Canada and Canadian Pacific. The original hotel opened in 1888, 110 years ago. Its location on the Canadian Pacific Railway's transcontinental line initially represented a convenient rest stop for travelers en route to or from the West Coast. It still performs this function but increasingly has attracted the international tourist seeking the experience of a night in a castle. In no small way, the commercial success of the Springs has been anchored to selling dreams and its great reputation has spread to the four corners of the globe. For the Banff Springs, the next 100 years promise to be every bit as exciting and rewarding as the last.

Robert S. DeMone
Chairman, President & C.E.O.
Canadian Pacific Hotels

FOREWORD

Photo: Mark Anthony Price

Declared a National Historic Site in 1988, the Banff Springs Hotel is a symbol of the unique history of the Canadian people and their longstanding and close relationship to the spectacular landscapes that make this country so special.

It has been a great honour to be one of a long and proud line of people who have had the privilege to manage this national heritage icon. In some ways, I must admit, it has seemed as much like managing a museum as a hotel. It is this realization that has been the greatest challenge and brought the greatest delight to me and to the management and employee teams upon whom I rely for our success at this hotel.

It is my sincerest hope that I, and those of my generation, will be judged by history to have respected the grand heritage of this great building. I hope too that those who follow after us will be able to use the hotel as a vehicle for experiencing the same glory as we felt in the national park landscape and that all who come will appreciate Canadian Pacific's important place in the evolving history of Canada's mountain West.

Edward D. Kissane
Vice President and General Manager
Banff Springs Hotel

The Banff Springs Hotel today at the foot of the Rockies. (CP)

A VISION

"The Banff Springs Hotel is absolutely palatial with the grandest view of mountain scenery we could ask to see, lying at our feet, the Valley of the Bow, hemmed in with its attendant mountains, a view that would repay a person for the whole journey" (Hart, 1983). These remarks by Reverend James Carmichael were part of an account of his 1888 trip written for friends in Great Britain. This account was later used by the Canadian Pacific in advertising literature for the hotel. Today, a hundred and ten years later, the description still holds true: it describes Banff Springs and the surrounding area perfectly.

The splendid stone hotel built by Walter E. Painter is still there, intact and grandiose. Additions through the years have been perfectly integrated to the original surviving building. As for the physical environment, it was protected as early as 1885 when the area was designated a national park. With the respect accorded by Canadian Pacific and the Canadian Parks Service, the Banff area is still the most unique mountain resort in Canada. Other parks have been created in the Rockies, the national parks of Jasper, Kootenay and Yoho, and the British Columbia provincial parks of Mount Robson, Mount Assiniboine and Hamber, forming one of the largest protected areas in the world.

The Banff Springs Hotel in 1920 photographed by Byron Harmon. (CP)

Building a Nation

At the time of the confederation in 1867, Canada as a nation was a tenuous proposition. Most of the country's population was in Ontario and Quebec. A great lone land extended to the West. A second large population was found in British territory on the Pacific coast. These people, however, were falling under the sway of the Americans. It was held that a true vision of nationhood could only emerge if Canada could expand to embrace the entire northern part of the continent in the manner in which the Americans had consolidated their nation.

In 1871, Ottawa promised British Columbia a railway if they agreed to enter the Canadian confederation. The offer was accepted though neither party had more than a vague notion of what it might cost or how much hard work it would be.

The extraordinary nature of this promise can only be made clear by comparing the Canadian situation with that of the United States when it constructed its first national railway. The United States had a population of more than 40 million people when it built its 2000 mile trans-continental line in 1869. That was ten times the population of Canada at the time.

A decade later, a country of 4 million people was proposing to build a rail line one and a half times longer than the American line. More than that, the Canadians had little idea where the line would go. The map of the West was a big blank filled with mountains and glaciers and gorges into which a train could drop and never be found. Still, the Canadians promised to build this railway in ten years!

The creation of the national railroad constituted the creation of Canada as we know it today as an entire Canadian civilization was carried West by the train. William Cornelius Van Horne not only built the railway, he was responsible in part for the developing identity of a nation.

ROBERT SANDFORD

The Canadian Pacific Railway played a unique role in opening up the Canadian wilderness to visitors from the world over. The railway also played a key role in supporting the creation of Canada's first national parks. The Banff Springs Hotel only occupies a minute portion of the 6,641 square kilometers taken up by Banff National Park but it was the building of this "great castle in the mountains" that truly launched tourism in the area. Railway history and the creation of the Canadian Pacific mountain hotels were sewn into the very fabric of Canada's national park system.

The Canadian Pacific empire-builders of a hundred years ago had a vision and those who came after have nurtured it, cherished it and kept it alive in all their endeavours to build a strong railway supported by a series of hotels, stations, cities, resorts, shiplines and even an airline.

The Banff Springs has been through a lot over all those years since Bruce Price designed the first CP hotel. First there were the golden years, but then came the 1929 depression, the closing of the hotel during the war, hard economic times, a second wind around 1980 and finally the boom of the 1990's. Without a doubt, it was the vision of the protagonists who figured in its remarkable saga that sustained the Banff Springs over its one hundred years. This remarkable vision was the legacy of William Van Horne and was so strong that it has endured to this day.

It is this vision that is presented here as we follow the events that reached their climax with the one hundredth birthday of the great Banff Springs Hotel.

The Banff Springs Hotel occupies a minute portion of the 6,641 square kilometers that make up the Banff National Park. This picture taken by Nicholas Morant in 1946 shows the hotel and the town of Banff across the Bow River. (CP)

"ALL I CAN SAY IS THAT THE WORK
HAS BEEN WELL DONE IN EVERY WAY."

WILLIAM CORNELIUS VAN HORNE

Train in Canadian Rockies, painting by M.V. Thornton. (CP)

CHAPTER I

The Last Spike

It was early morning on a cold and rainy day in November 1885, in a lonely spot between Sicamous and Revelstoke in the Monashee Mountains. For this young country, the event that was taking place was the most important of the whole decade, if not the century. Here at Craigellachie in Eagle Pass the last spike was being driven into the railway line linking the eastern shores to the west coast of a great country, Canada.

The blows that drove the iron home reverberated throughout the Empire. The nine provinces of Canada were now united, making one nation. They brought Yokohama several hundred miles nearer to Liverpool and London. They enabled the merchants of Montreal and Toronto to stretch out and grasp the products of the valleys of the Fraser and the Columbia and trade directly with the tea-growers and silk-weavers of Japan and

CPR work camp, 1884. In 4 years and 6 months 30,000 labourers built the railway — French and English, Scots and Irish, Italians and Slavs, Swedes and Yankees, Canadians and Chinese. (CP)

China. They opened up new and greater markets to the farmers of Manitoba and the colonists on the Pacific Coast for their crops, their coal, their forests, their fish and their ore.

Pierre Berton, who has written numerous books on the saga of the CPR, describes this moment in *The Last Spike*:

> The very simplicity and spontaneity of the scene at Eagle Pass, the lack of pomp, the absence of oratory, the plainness of the crowd, the presence of the workmen in the foreground, made the spectacle an oddly memorable one.

It was a dull, murky November morning, the tall mountains sheathed the clouds, the dark firs and cedars dripping in a coverlet of wet snow. Up puffed the quaint engine with its polished brass boiler, its cordwood fender, its diamond-shaped smokestack and the great square box in front containing the acetylene headlight on whose glass was painted the number 148. The ceremonial party descended and walked though the clearing of stumps and debris to the spot where Major Rogers was holding the tie bar under the final rail. The oldest director present, Donald A. Smith, was chosen to drive the last spike. Smith posed with the uplifted hammer. The assembly froze. The shutter clicked. Smith lowered the hammer onto the spike. There was absolute silence, then the spell was broken by an extraordinary cheer.

Donald A. Smith driving the last spike in the railway linking east and west on November 7, 1885, referred to as the Great Canadian Photograph. (CP)

A simple ceremony, because the general manager of the company, William Van Horne, wanted it that way. On his orders, all the working men and navvies available were gathered there that day as Donald Smith struck the last spike. Behind the general manager, who had arrived in Canada 46 months earlier, now stretched twin ribbons of steel 2,905 miles (or 4,648 km) long. The accomplishment of this day might well have called for a eulogy commending the men behind this incredible undertaking and a recollection of the turmoil that had prevailed all along the line, the opposition of so many governments and so many individuals and the extraordinary solutions that had been found to the multitude of problems that had arisen. But William Van Horne was not a speaker and his was the only speech to underline this extraordinary event which so many had believed should never come about. It was brief and to the point: "All I can say is that the work has been well done in every way".

The Canadian Pacific Railway Company "CPR Syndicate" was formed in February 1881 by Donald Smith, George Stephen, Duncan MacIntyre and James Hill. The company was granted a charter and George Stephen became the first president. The CPR Syndicate was backed financially by three brokerage firms from New York, London and Paris. It was this syndicate that hired William Van Horne as general manager of the Canadian Pacific Railway.

Not only would Van Horne's vision of the CPR "spanning the world" become a reality but the Canadian Pacific Railway also expanded around the world by sea and later by plane bringing tourists to Canada. (Early poster from The Selling of Canada. CP)

William Van Horne

William Cornelius Van Horne was born in Chelsea, Illinois. His father was a lawyer and the first Justice of the Peace for the district. At the age of 15, Van Horne was hired as a freight checker on the Michigan Central Railway, starting an amazing career in the rail business. Back then, his goal was to become general superintendent so that he could ride to work in a personal car. He attained this goal at the age of 28 and before his 30th birthday he was appointed general manager of the St. Louis, Kansas City and Northern Railway. It was as general superintendent of the Chicago, Milwaukee and St. Paul Railway that he attracted the interest of James Jerome Hill, the most successful railroad king in US history. From him, Van Horne learned of the ambitious plans for a railway in Canada. He was 38 years old when he assumed his duties as general manager of the Canadian Pacific on December 31, 1881. Van Horne was a man of extraordinary vision. He also was blessed with the determination it took to make his vision come true, laying twenty-nine hundred miles of track across a barely explored continent.

William Cornelius Van Horne was the driving force behind this giant enterprise. This "man of iron" saw it through with the help of the sheer force of his will, his strength of character, his extraordinary physical presence and his charisma. (CP)

Van Horne became a dominant force in the world of Canadian finance, sitting on the boards of 30 major corporations. Upon his retirement from the Canadian Pacific Railway on June 12, 1899, he found time to build railroads across Cuba and Guatemala.

Van Horne's interests were diversified and included paleontology, geology, art, painting and architecture. He was an avid art collector and *connoisseur* and his two hundred paintings included works by Turner, Hogarth, El Greco, Renoir, Rubens, Titian, Murrillo, Rembrandt, Goya, Da Vinci, Franz Halls and Velasquez. He possessed the largest collection of Japanese pottery in North America and it is said that he could correctly identify nine out of ten oriental ceramic objects while blindfolded. This true "renaissance man" was also a horticulturist. He grew peaches and kept vineyards at his island summer estate near St. Andrews, New Brunswick, which he named "Covenhoven". He also raised prize cattle in New Brunswick and Selkirk, Manitoba.

Upon Van Horne's death in September 1915, the entire Canadian Pacific system was halted in silent homage for five minutes across the continent. Cuba declared a day of national mourning. The country lost one of its most valuable Canadians as his private coach the "Saskatchewan" carried him for burial to Joliet, Illinois, his ancestral home.

As Peter Newman wrote in 1959: "Few men have nourished such flamboyant ambitions and even fewer have lived to witness their fulfillment".

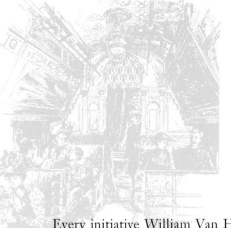

Every initiative William Van Horne and Sandford Fleming undertook between 1881 and that day in 1885 at Craigellachie was aimed at creating a railway line powerful enough to bring together the east and the west in Canada. Trains, Pullman cars, freight, bridges, stations, hotels and numerous cities had to be invented by these two powerful men to complete this railway line.

At the time the railway was completed, Van Horne's mind was fixed on immediate problems: building the Vancouver train station, creating the Pacific postal service and building the Atlantic Steamship line. Looking beyond the opening of the railway line, he envisioned a fleet of white Empress passenger liners, château-style hotels from coast to coast and the international slogan proclaiming that the CPR "spanned" the world.

Van Horne's vision was centered on the railway and it reflected Sandford Fleming's dream expressed at the site of Rogers Pass in September 1883: "I asked myself if this solitude would be unchanged or whether civilization in some form of its complex requirements would ever penetrate this region... It cannot be that this immense valley will remain the haunt of a few wild animals... How soon will a busy crowd of workmen take possession of these solitudes, and the steam whistle echo and re-echo where now all is silent? In the ages to come how many trains will run to and from sea to sea with millions of passengers?" (Berton, 1971).

Crow Foot

Back in the 1880's after a treaty with the Blackfeet tribe had been signed and about the time the Canadian Pacific Railway was pushing its lines of steel into the west, Chief Crow Foot had become known to William Van Horne, then general manager of the Canadian Pacific. Crow Foot could have stopped the railway but he forbore to take up arms. As a token of the esteem held for the famous chief he was presented with a perpetual pass over the Railway Company's lines. This pass became Crow Foot's most treasured possession and he exhibited it with pride. (CP)

Drawing of dining car interior in 1895: fresh flowers, sterling silver, upholstered seats and impressive service. (Hart, E.J., The Selling of Canada)

MOUNT STEPHEN HOUSE.

BANFF HOTEL

THE GLACIER HOUSE

Office Banff Springs Hotel

Brochure for the first CPR hotels in the west: Mount Stephen House, Glacier House, Hotel Vancouver and the Banff Springs. (CP)

As early as 1886, the "railroad general" William Van Horne envisioned wealthy Europeans and Americans touring the Canadian Rockies, climbing its peaks and exploring its rivers and gorges. In order to maintain control over the quality of passenger service, Van Horne decided that the CPR would own all its sleeping, parlour and dining cars from the outset. Many of these cars were built by Barney & Smith Co of Dayton, Ohio.

But it was Van Horne himself who designed the cars and saw to their interior decor. Under his guidance, the advertising for the dining car service was extravagant: "The Canadian Pacific Railway Dining Cars excel in elegance of design and furniture and in the quality of food and attendance anything hitherto offered to transcontinental travellers. The fare provided in these cars is the best procurable and the cooking has a wide reputation for excellence. Local delicacies such as trout, prairie hens, antelope steaks, Fraser River salmon succeed one another as the train moves westward. The wines are of the company's special importation and are of the finest quality." The price for these meals was seventy-five cents!

It was impracticable, however, to haul the heavy dining cars over the steepest grades of the mountains. Some sort of meal service had to be provided for travellers who made stops in the wilderness so the railway built alpine resorts at three locations: Mount Stephen House at Field in the Kicking Horse Valley, Glacier House at the foot of Illecillewaet Glacier near the summit of Rogers Pass and the Fraser Canyon House at North Bend. These three chalet-like dining stations were designed by Thomas Charles Sorby, the same architect who built the Hotel Vancouver for the railway line. With the help of advertising tourism flourished in these three locations.

Van Horne had special plans for tourism development in the West. He planned a national park, a series of grand hotels, modest hotels, small Swiss chalets, railway stations of all sizes and gave orders to an army of people destined to make the dream come true. He actualized this vision through methodical organization and an iron will. His plans for developing the Rockies included a protected area, where nature and wildlife would be preserved for all time. In 1883, Van Horne suggested that a national park be created around Lac des Arcs.

Two years later, in 1885, Van Horne's national park dreams were realized when a small area around a series of hot springs were set aside as Canada's first nature reserve. The reserve was expanded in 1887 and later became Banff National Park.

The first-class cars were the most luxurious of the time. (CP)

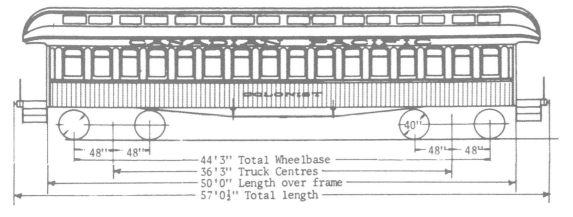

48" | 48"
44'3" Total Wheelbase
36'3" Truck Centres
50'0" Length over frame
57'0½" Total length
40"
48" | 48"

Van Horne designed the cars and saw to their interior decor. (CP)

The Creation of the National Parks

The first attempt at a reservation for park purposes was made rather late in the autumn of 1883, probably in November of that year, by Sir William Van Horne, immediately after he saw the territory along the C.P.R. west of Calgary.

WILLIAM PEARCE

Commissioner
Department of the Interior
Government of Canada
(In a speech to the Historical Society of Calgary, 1924)

The Birth of a Park

The discovery of caves and mineral waters near Banff marked the origin of the first Canadian national park.

In the fall of 1883, the main line of the Canadian Pacific Railway had been laid to within a few kilometres of Kicking Horse Pass, a narrow saddle on the Great Divide that separates waters that flow into the Pacific from those that flow into the Atlantic at Hudson Bay. Siding 29 was laid on October 27th, 1883 — one of the last tasks before concluding work for the season. Many of the men on the construction teams had heard tales of mysterious vapors rising through the forest on the far side of Bow River so a few of them decided to investigate in early November. They built a raft and crossed the river to the foot of Terrace Mountain. On November 8, 1883, three young men, Franklin McCabe and brothers William and Thomas McCardell found a rock basin filled with hot, steamy, odorous water at the base of a small cliff on Terrace Mountain (known today as Sulphur Mountain). Above was a cave opening. They built a ladder to descend into the hot pool below ground and built a fence around their cave. On another occasion, they "discovered" a spring higher up in the mountain. McCardell described the find as "some fantastic dream from a tale of the Arabian Nights".

Early photograph of the springs near Banff. (CP)

The sulphur pool in full operation at the Banff "Cave and Basin". (CP)

Starting their very own "spa" business, they built a rough shack beside their cave and invited fellow workers and locals to soak in the warm waters. Although these enterprising individuals ran their "Cave and Basin" operation in 1884 and 1885, they were never allowed a claim by the federal government. The government declared the springs a federal reserve at the same time it created Banff National Park.

Back in the fall of 1883, another historic moment occured. William Cornelius Van Horne, at a meeting of the directors of the Canadian Pacific Railway, named the area adjacent to the Bow River near the site of Siding 29. He named it Banff, after Banffshire in Scotland, the ancestral home of railway financiers George Stephen and Donald Smith. He also, during the same period of time, made his first attempt to convince the government to create a reserve for park purposes.

A Dominion Land Surveyor named William Pearce was sent from Ottawa. He advised the government to take control of the Sulphur Mountain area. On November 28, 1885, an Order in Council was passed making just over 26 square kilometres on the north slopes of Sulphur Mountain Canada's first national park.

And so it was that railway history and the birth of Canadian Pacific Hotels were sewn into the very fabric of Canada's national park system.

In the beginning, the springs in the town of Banff were not reserved for the Canadian Pacific alone. At the turn of the century, the medicinal properties of "the waters" were attracting interest all over the world and resorts such as Baden-Baden, Evian-les-Bains and Saratoga Springs were drawing thousands of visitors. The early history of American resorts is intimately linked to the quest for restorative and healing waters, much like that of the Europeans as shown at Bath and Evian, and there are quite a few spring resorts in Pennsylvania, Virginia and, of course, Saratoga Springs, New York. It was not long before the word spread that hot springs had been discovered in the Rockies and many investors followed in the steps of the Canadian Pacific and opened spas or medical resorts.

A sanitarium was built in 1886 by Dr. Robert Q. Brett. At his hotel/hospital, Dr. Brett treated patients with the waters from the Upper Hot Springs. This sanitarium, Grandview Villa, was built adjacent to the springs and it prospered for a few years. When the building burned down in 1901, the government canceled all the leases on the springs and took over the operation of the basin and Upper Hot Springs.

Van Horne decided that it would be a good idea to build his grand hotel as close as possible to the sulphur springs. It was the famous railway guide Tom Wilson who first took the general manager to the spot where the hotel stands. There are some who say that Van Horne was tired of hiking through the dense bush after Wilson and sat down in view of the Bow River. According to this version, he decided to go no further so the spot was found.

At the future Banff Springs Hotel, under Van Horne's supervision, two pools were to be built which were later described as "the finest bathing establishment on the continent". The indoor pool measured 28 ft x 80 ft and contained the warm sulphurous water piped through wooden pipes directly from the hot springs on Sulphur Mountain. This water was kept at an average temperature of 90 degrees fahrenheit. The outdoor pool was filled with cold water. In addition, the facilities included Turkish and Russian baths in marble.

The sulphur springs were one of the main attractions of the Canadian Pacific hotel. Parks Canada is now operating the Upper Hot Springs and the Cave and Basin for the tourists. The hotel has kept the tradition of offering mineral baths to its guests, however, as we will see further on.

The first Banff Springs Hotel as illustrated on a company pamphlet 1895-1898. (CP)

CHAPTER II

The First Hotel

1888 to 1899

During all those years he was busy constructing a railway through the mountains, Van Horne dreamed of building a grand European-style hotel designed to be a jewel in the crown of the magnificent natural setting of the Rockies. Walter Vaughan, Van Horne's biographer, tells us how he took a personal interest in everything he was responsible for: "Van Horne began to realize a long-held dream of starting a system of picturesque hotels commanding the choicest view of the mountains. He always involved himself in sketching, suggesting and modifying the plans of these structures."

To build this "castle" in the Rockies, William Van Horne needed an architect of exceptional ability, capable of integrating a huge building with the surrounding forests. He found just the man for the job: a brilliant New Yorker named Bruce Price who had studied under the world-renowned Henry Hobson Richardson.

Van Horne had become aware of Bruce Price through a remarkable series of interviews in which the architect had given his philosophy for building a house in the country. Price's view of the relationship of structure to landscape mirrored Van Horne's: "The first thing for the architect to keep in mind in designing a country house is not going

Portrait of Bruce Price, the American architect who designed the Banff Springs Hotel. (CP)

Bruce Price's original sketch for the CPR hotel at Banff. The completed hotel was slightly different. (Cornell Library Archives)

17

My Dear Mr. VanHorn.
I send herewith a sketch
and plans of proposed
Hotel at Banff. which if
nothing else will afford a
basis to construct a proper
plan upon.
I think the perspective
and plans will sufficiently
explain themselves.
There are 92 masters rooms
and 18 servants Rooms.
The Kitchen wing is intended
to be a frame and sheathed one
story structure built in the
most economical manner.

Letter from Bruce Price to William Van Horne, Sept. 25, 1886. (CP)

Many letters from Bruce Price to Van Horne bear witness to the architect's desire to please his client:

I send herewith a sketch and plans of the proposed Hotel at Banff... There are 92 master rooms and 18 steward rooms. The kitchen wing is intended to be a frame and sheathed one story structure built in the most economical manner. The heating and its plant and fuel bins could be placed under the Dining Room...
(Bruce Price to Van Horne, Sept. 25, 1886, CPR Archives)

in opposition to nature... A house is but a part of a scene, and the more complete the scene, the more naturally the house is adapted to its surroundings, the better it fits into the landscape, the better the result... It is so easy to invent, and so extremely difficult to design." Van Horne asked Price to produce drawings and designs for a luxurious hotel for the site of Banff. At the time, Bruce Price was completing plans for the Canadian Pacific Railway station in Montreal.

The design by the American architect was reminiscent of the shingle style mansions gracing the New England coast at such places as Bar Harbor, Newport, with their long roofs punctuated with dormers, oriel windows corbelled out from the wall, high chimneys, many asymmetrical facades and hanging dormers.

The original Banff Springs Hotel as seen from the Bow River, 1888. Photographed by Boorne & May, Calgary. (CP)

"The house does not stand out in the land-scape, but fits in with it," Bruce Price had written, and the design of the Banff Hotel did indeed fit the landscape in which it was built. The exterior veneer suggested cream coloured Winnipeg brick. Pointed dormers, corner turrets and large oriels accentuated the roofs. The wooden building with its asymmetrical roofline and accentuated facade was in harmony with the mountains in which it was nestled.

Set in the majestic mountains, the chateau blended with the panoramas. It was built of wood with five stories designed in the shape of an H and a wing extending towards the Bow River. Outside the verandas provided visual access to the mountains. Inside a large central hall occupied most of the ground floor.

An anecdote recorded by Van Horne's biographer Walter Vaughan reveals the undivided attention which Van Horne gave to the construction of the Banff Springs Hotel. It also shows that Bruce Price did not personally supervise the job:

> The builder turned the hotel the wrong side about, giving the kitchen the finest outlook on the magnificent panorama of the Bow Valley. Van Horne arrived and saw the blunder. His wrath amply illustrated the description of a colleague: "Van Horne was one of the most considerate and even tempered of men, but when an explosion came, it was magnificent." However, by the time the cyclone had spent itself a remedy was forthcoming. He sketched a rotunda pavilion on the spot, and ordered it to be erected so as to secure the coveted view for the guests.

The pavilion designed by Van Horne, overlooking the Fairholme Range, circa 1890. By Boorne and May, Calgary. (CP)

Despite its rustic-looking exterior, the building had "modern" conveniences such as steam heat, electric lighting, elevators, a reading room, several parlors, dining rooms and a smoking room. The most outstanding feature of the luxurious hotel was the octagonal Great Hall five stories high in the core of the building. In this open space, overhanging balconies on all floors allowed an uninterrupted view of the main lobby. Five stories of rooms were built into the wings. A very large dining room was accompanied on the ground floor by smoking rooms, a reading room, a billiard room and a bar. For evening entertainment, an impressive ballroom was also created.

The red pine galleries overlooking the rotunda in the
first Banff Springs Hotel,
1888. (CP)

The hotel originally accommodated
280 visitors and the nearby bath house provided 10 rooms and a swimming pool. Need-
less to say, the pavilion overlooking the Bow
River was the most romantic extension of the
entire hotel. There were reproduction antiques
manufactured in Montreal and paintings of
European significance which enhanced the
atmosphere and enticed the wealthy to what
was regarded as a jewel in the remote wilderness of the Canadian Rockies.

The Banff Springs Hotel opened in June of
1888 with George Holiday as manager. Rates
were $3.50 per night, with a summer season
from May 15th to October 1st. Van Horne's
assertion at the opening ceremony that it was
"the finest hotel on the North American continent" underscored the CPR's intention to
establish a world-famous resort catering to an
international clientele.

The entire hotel complex had cost a quarter of a million to build. Van Horne's philosophy ("Since we can't export the scenery, we
will have to import the tourists") had set Banff
tourism on its way. The eager Van Horne created a massive campaign to lure European and

American visitors and succeeded in making the Banff Springs Hotel one of the most sought-after resorts in the world. He personally saw to all the details of the advertising designed to entice wealthy tourists to the wilderness of the Canadian Rockies. He even asked the best artists of the day to provide paintings of Canadian scenery to adorn his railway coaches and promotional material, thus driving Canadian art toward new standards.

In its first season in 1888, the hotel was a great success. The Banff Springs Hotel register shows that there were 1,503 guests that year, 801 of whom were from Canada, 389 from the United States, 289 from Great Britain and 24 from other countries. One of the first guests was Lady Agnes MacDonald, the wife of Canada's first Prime Minister, who had fallen under the spell of the Rockies while on a transcontinental trip in 1886. She later occupied a log cabin built by Harry Brathwaite Abbott adjacent to the hotel. Earnscliffe cottage became her summer home for 1887, 1888 and 1889. It is still standing after over a hundred years.

View of a section of Agnes MacDonald's wooden cottage Earnscliffe. Despite the rustic-looking exterior it has been restored with all the modern conveniences. It is currently the home of the general manager and his family. (Photo: Mark Anthony Price, 1996)

Just a few years later, in 1905, the register featured the names of guests from South Africa, the Hague, Paris, Austria, England, Japan, the United States, Borneo, Hong Kong and, of course, the rest of Canada. Van Horne's tourism dream was coming true!

In an 1899 pamphlet designed with overseas visitors in mind, the hotel was touted as follows:

> Banff the Beautiful: there is not a more fascinating resort on all this continent than the Banff Springs Hotel, on the line of the Canadian Pacific Railway, in the heart of the Rocky Mountains... The very acme of sublimity and grandeur is reached, and in its natural beauty, Banff finds no fitting rival in other lands.

The guests at the Banff Springs Hotel took part in swimming, golfing, hiking, climbing and canoeing activities or just plain admired and enjoyed the scenery. With this very first castle in the mountains, Van Horne set the tone for all the future hotels along the railway line. Rarefied elegance, romantic decor, a hushed atmosphere, exceptional dining and impeccable service were to be the rule for the exclusive and aristocratic clientele.

Original bill for Mr. L.W. Briggs, dated July 20th, 1895. (CPH)

Nicholas Morant was the most famous of the official railway photographers. This photograph was taken in 1951.

The Canadian government actively encouraged Canadian Pacific to involve itself in the widespread promotion of Canada's national parks as tourist attractions. Canadian Pacific was encouraged to provide that help by employing its extensive advertising network to bring visitors from abroad to pay for the growing system of natural reserves in Canada.

Part of the appeal of early Canadian Pacific advertising was elegant graphic design. Another component was fine photography. Early photographic images of the mountain west became the first examples of photography as an art form. Canadian Pacific developed a close and lasting relationship with photographers of the calibre of William Notman and son of Montreal and with other early photographic houses. Once the railway

was completed, however, it created its own photographic department. The most famous of the official railway photographers was Nicholas Morant. Morant was born in Kamloops in 1910 and began working in the publicity department of the railway in 1929. For the next forty-four years, Morant captured the mood of an entire country that owed its livelihood, if not its very existence, to the Canadian Pacific Railroad.

Early Canadian Pacific promotion has played a major role in Canadian culture. The sophisticated marketing strategies employed by the railway to attract visitors to the remote west set the standard for a uniquely Canadian approach to advertising. The image CP created of itself gradually became the image of the West.

ROBERT SANDFORD

The Birth of Western Art

Though early advertising depicted the Rockies by way of black and white engravings and were largely based on photographs, many were stunning works of art. When the railway was completed, the CPR began to hire more artists to interpret the grandeur of the mountain west. Famous early Canadian painters like Lucius O'Brien, F.M. Bell-Smith and Marmeduke Matthews created masterpieces of the mountains surrounding railway hotels at Banff, Lake Louise, Field and Rogers Pass.

These ground breaking artists established the visual traditions that make landscape painting a vital part of Canadian Rockies culture today. By contracting the best artists to illustrate their promotional materials, Canadian Pacific drove Canadian art toward new standards of local authenticity.

After railway tourism established Banff and Lake Louise as international destinations, a great number of very competent artists made their way independently to the Rockies or painted the grand scenery in the employ of the Canadian Pacific Railway.

The works originally found in the CP's mountain hotels and in the railway's archives rank among the finest pieces by the best artists in Canada. They include the works of Nina Crumrine, Stanley Turner, Langdon Kihn and Lila Dicken. Artists of the calibre of Carl Rungius, Belmore Browne, A.C. Leighton, Walter Phillips and Nicholas de Grandmaison were also supported at various times in their lives by commissions from Canadian Pacific Hotels. These artists developed the foundation for pictorial art in the West and continue to shape the way we think about ourselves in relation to where we live. There is not a single successful contemporary landscape artist in Alberta who does not in some way owe part of their success to earlier artists who worked in the employ of Canadian Pacific.

ROBERT SANDFORD

Painting by Peter Whyte "Yoho Valley Bungalow Camp", 1930. To promote the Rockies in Europe, Van Horne commissioned the best Canadian painters. (CP)

Indeed the Banff Springs was widely acclaimed as the finest hotel in North America and declared to be a "public pleasure ground" without equal. Streams had been spanned, roads laid out and trails cut, penetrating miles into the wilderness, so that in several directions visitors could drive, ride or wander, breathing in the exhilarating mountain air or seeking out the best spots for brush, pencil or camera. The promotional pamphlet also extolled the virtues of the medicinal hot springs and raved about the Lakes in the Clouds, Lake Louise, Mirror Lake and Lake Agnes which could be reached on foot, ponies or with the help of mountain guides.

Poster promoting mountain climbing in the Rockies. (CP)

PACIFIC COAST ·TOURS· THROUGH·THE CANADIAN ·PACIFIC· ROCKIES

Mountain Climbers, painting by Carl Rungius. (CP)

There was truly something for everyone:

Guests find amusement in croquet, lawn tennis, billiards, bowling etc... in addition to driving, fishing, boating, bathing and mountain climbing. In the hotel, a dark room has been furnished for the use of photographers... Alpenstocks for mountain climbers can be purchased at Banff, Lake Louise and Glacier, at each of which places there are facilities for branding upon them the names of the different peaks in their neighbourhood, thus converting the staffs into interesting souvenirs. The hotel rates are from $3.50 to $5.00 per day, a moderate charge for such a hotel in such a locality.

(CPR Archives)

The Challenge of the Mountains was a spectacular CPR booklet featuring Alpine Annie in the Canadian Rockies. (CP)

The Challenge of the Mountains

The Challenge of the Mountains

To bring tourists to his railway line, William Van Horne used the lure of the Canadian Rockies. European and American alpinists came to the Selkirks and Glacier House where he offered them an elegant hostelry, good food and unclimbed mountains. Thanks to the CPR's effective advertising and the pamphlets it distributed around the world, climbers from the most famous alpine clubs flocked to the Canadian ranges. In July of 1887 the affluent Philadelphian George Vaux and his family arrived at Glacier House as part of a transcontinental CPR rail adventure. Over the next 40 years, the Vaux family would make a significant contributions to photography and glacier research in the Selkirks and the Rocky Mountains.

Guests were invited to try out a teepee. This famous photograph was taken by Byron Harmon in 1924. It became so popular that a teepee was put up on the shores of Bow Lake for many years. (Whyte Museum of the Canadian Rockies)

Climbers on Mount Resplendent west of Jasper. This photograph by Byron Harmon was taken during an Alpine Club climb in 1913. (Whyte Museum of the Canadian Rockies)

Walter Fuez and Rudolph Aemmer, ready to guide guests to the high peaks of the Rockies. (CP)

(23 years later), president Arthur Oliver Wheeler named Sir Sandford Fleming honorary president.

An important tradition of the Alpine Club was the annual mountaineering camp, the first of which took place in July 1906. This tradition eventually turned Canada into one of the world's foremost mountain climbing nations. The focus of the Club activities was in Banff, in a clubhouse on Sulphur Mountain Road. (In 1972 the clubhouse was demolished at the request of Parks Canada and rebuilt in Canmore.)

For the ordinary tourist, mountain climbing in the Rockies was a hazardous business to say the least, with no proper guides, no guide books and no shelters in the wilderness. Vice-president Shaughnessy became quickly aware of the dangers and wired London about the possibility of hiring Swiss guides for the CP. In 1899, two qualified guides from Interlaken arrived in Montreal. It is said that their first year at Glacier House was less filled with climbing than promotional work, posing for pictures next to delighted tourists.

Members of the Appalachian Mountain Club from the US competed with people from the British Alpine Club to be the first to accomplish climbs in the Rockies. In the summer of 1883 Fleming, accompanied by George Munro (Dean of Queen's University), Major A.B. Rogers and his nephew Albert, reached the Rogers Pass summit. Amazed by the extraordinary panorama of peaks in the Rockies, Fleming decided on the spot that Canada needed an alpine Club, naming his friends as founding members of the institution. At the first meeting of the ACC in March 1906

A great deal of advertising literature was published by the CP but the most popular was a pamphlet called "The Challenge of the Mountains". It was published at the beginning of 1900, just as the railway company was embarking on a remarkable program of hiking, horseback riding, climbing and touring in the Rockies.

It was inevitable that the Rockies would become the new popular playground. Most of the approximately 1100 peaks which surrounded the railway lines were unknown and unclimbed. A climbers' elite of Europeans and Americans, tired of the Matterhorns and the Mont Blancs, rushed west to the Selkirks and the Rockies.

Georgia Englehard climbing in the Rockies. (CP)

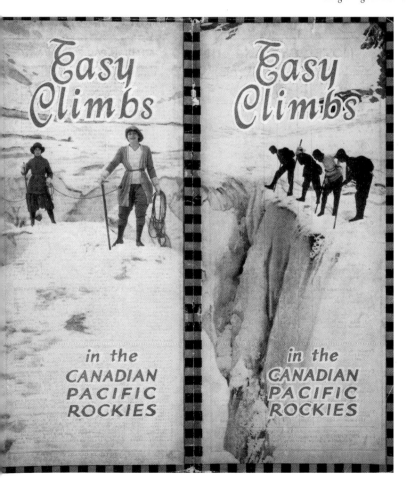

"After establishing a Canadian Rockies mountain climbing record of thirty-eight (38) high peaks in one season, Miss Georgia Englehard, 24 year old alpinist from New York City, left the Banff Springs Hotel for home October 15. Since May 25, she in company with Ernest Fuez, Swiss guide stationed at Château Lake Louise, had made some of the difficult ascents in the Mountains. She climbed 24 peaks in the Selkirks, the difficult Chancellor Peak (10,731 ft) in Yoho Park and Mt Victoria (11,355 ft) at Lake Louise. Her last two weeks before departure were spent at Mt. Assiniboine Camps with a view of conquering this "Matterhorn" of American Mt. Assiniboine (11,850 ft)" (CPR News, 1932).

The brochure "Easy Climbs in the Canadian Pacific Rockies" aimed to attract neophyte alpinists. Published in the early 1900's. (CP)

The "castle in winter" as it could be seen by 1928 and as it still is today. (CPH)

A Castle is Born
1900 to 1928

In 1899, William Van Horne, who had been president of the company since 1888, tendered his resignation, leaving the CPR in the capable hands of Sir Thomas Shaughnessy. Shaughnessy had been assistant general manager since 1885.

By the turn of the century, the hotel was one of the most popular in North America. It became apparent that the Banff Springs would have to be enlarged if it was to accommodate all those wishing to stay there. The rapid expansion of the hotel's clientele and ever present difficulty getting funds for the renovation program resulted in a long period of building projects. For the sake of clarity hotel development can be divided into 2 periods: 1900 to 1910 when changes were made to the original 1888 building and 1910 to 1928 when all alterations were part of the design for a "new hotel".

In 1902-1903 a new wing similar to the original wing gave the hotel a north-south orientation. This new wing was joined to the other one by a wooden passageway. (CP)

BANFF SPRINGS HOTEL.

A concrete centre tower, large wings with smaller towers, terraces, pools, towers and pavilion were all part of the elegant plan. Drawing by Walter Painter. (CP)

Major additions were made to the hotel in 1903, 1904 and 1905. The most extensive of these was the half-million construction project of 1902-03: the construction of a whole new wing similar to the original one and joined to it by a wooden passageway (this passageway served as a buffer in case of fire). Historian Bart Robinson gives us a description of the interior:

It is finished in native wood — Douglas fir — every piece of which has gone through the hands of artistic workers. The ceiling and other decorations have been put on in accord with perfect harmony, and the electric lights — well, thousands have been spent on them. The parlours, the sleeping rooms, retreats, refreshment booths, verandahs, baths, and all such are modern and luxurious to the limit.

After the building of the wing, large additions were put up in 1904 and 1905, possibly the two six-storey framed towers. (Precise dates and details for renovations between 1900 and 1910 are unfortunately few and far between.) Then in the winter of 1906 through 1907, some 70 men worked on a new addition to the southeast part of the hotel which housed the boiler, engine and laundry rooms.

After the hectic 1910 and 1911 seasons, when 22,000 guests occupied the hotel in one summer, it became evident to the CPR that a new building had to be added to the site. An American architect and disciple of Bruce Price, Walter S. Painter was chosen to design a new hotel for Banff. He had been working for the Canadian Pacific as chief architect since 1905.

Some of his projects included the Château Lake Louise and Hotel Vancouver and the Painter wing at the Château Frontenac.

In a series of plans, Painter proposed replacing the old wood structure with a concrete and steel building characterized by a large eleven-storey concrete centre tower 70 feet wide and 200 feet tall. The tower was flanked on each side by large wings ending in smaller towers. The CPR accepted Painter's proposal but decided to do the work in stages.

By early spring 1912, the completion of the centre wing — a first step in the construction of the "new" hotel — included two swimming pools in front of the hotel. Bart Robinson gives an excellent description in *The Story of a Hotel:*

Walter S. Painter

Walter S. Painter was born in Reading, Pennsylvania in 1877. He came to Canada in 1901 and designed the Russell Theatre in Ottawa, the auditorium and opera house in Quebec City, a theatre in London, Ontario and a number of theatres in the United States. In 1905 he was named chief architect for the CPR. Among his accomplishments were the Montreal and Vancouver hotels, several train stations and the Empress Hotel in Victoria. He enlarged the Hotel Palliser in Calgary and also designed the Banff Cave and Basin swimming pools and buildings. Painter later returned to Banff, where he retired in 1957.

The "establishment" consisted of three terraces. The outer and lower one was a semi-circular cold, fresh-water pool, while the second terrace held a warm sulphur pool... separated from the outer pool by a graceful loggia. The second terrace also contained complete Turkish and Russian baths with no less than 100 individual dressing rooms... The third and final terrace consisted of cooling rooms, private sulphur baths, and rooms for an imported Swedish masseur, while the roof to the third terrace functioned as a wide promenade.

In 1914, the centre tower with its centre wing housed a large dining room, a rotunda that was the lobby and bedrooms for 300 guests; it also included three terraces. The hotel kept its two wooden wings until 1925. (CP)

*Sketch of the great
courtyard at the Banff
Springs in an advertising
brochure. (CP)*

The centre tower was completed by May of 1914, replacing the old passageway connecting the two wings. It was faced with Mount Rundle limestone quarried nearby and installed by Italian stone cutters and Scottish masons, making the exterior decor compatible with its mountainous surroundings. This tower housed a large dining room, a rotunda that was the lobby and bedrooms for 300 guests. It was a remarkable work of art praised by everyone.

Over two million dollars were spent on Painter's centre portion where one could find the new interiors designed by Mrs. Kate Reed, wife of manager Hayter Reed. These elegant interiors enhanced by wicker furniture are a credit to the talent of Mrs. Reed who was also

responsible for the interior design at many of the CPR's other hotels, including the famous Château Frontenac. The dark wainscotting, the coffered ceiling, the sculpted decors and the Persian rugs created a romantic atmosphere under the glow of chandeliers and wall sconces. The floors were enhanced by red English tiles and the comfort and elegance of each and every room was at a par with the new decor of the Palliser in Calgary and the Château Frontenac in Quebec City.

The Reception Hall in the late 1920's, shown here in its original appearance, with its dark wood panelling and its buffalo head. (CP)

Mrs Hayter Reed was responsible for the interior design until the late 1920's. The sun parlour, enhanced by wicker furniture. (CP)

The hotel was known for its fine bathing. This is the semi-circular fresh water pool, built around 1911. The wooden north wing can be seen more closely here. (CP)

The railway company then decided to "sit back a bit and see how things went". A decade later it became obvious that more new facilities needed to be built to lodge the hundreds of guests who had to be turned away from the hotel every summer. With the Painter Tower in place, architect J.W. Orrock redesigned the whole hotel in a greater and more monumental style, with both wings much larger than those in Painter's design. The new wings were to be constructed in two consecutive winters, 1926-27 and 1927-28.

To accommodate the guests during the replacement of the first wing, a 100-room Tudor style building was built during the winter of 1925-26. Work was about to begin on the south wing when, on April 6th, 1926, a fire burned down the old 1888 northerly oriented wooden wing. The new wing in steel and stone was completed by the spring of 1927, less than a year after the fire. At the end of the 1926 hotel season, the south wing had been pulled down. Construction work began in September 1927 and was completed within seven months. The Banff Springs as we know it today was designed by Walter Painter and by J.W. Orrock.

The north wing on fire,
April 6th, 1926. (CP)

The interior of the Painter tower
was badly damaged. (CP)

The north wing on fire.
(Whyte Museum of the Canadian Rockies)

Construction of the south
wing. The work began at
the end of the 1927
season and lasted seven
months. (CP)

A castle was born! The "new" Banff Springs Hotel opened on May 15, 1928. It was praised the world over for its château-like structure in stone, topped with steep copper roofs punctuated with turrets, finials, dormers and oriels. The importance of the event was underlined by the fact that a number of people from the CPR, including the president Sir Edward Beatty himself, were there for the opening ceremonies.

The wondrous "castle" in the Scottish baronial tradition had walls six feet thick, great rooms filled with treasures and heirlooms and a huge banquet hall. The 1935 CPR pamphlet *Castle in the Air* described it as "a haven of gracious living in a setting of breath-taking beauty, where visitors from all over the world return year after year; for, once visited, Banff Springs calls again."

The final concept of the Banff Springs Hotel was slightly different from the Painter design. For example, the wings are much larger. (CP)

A castle was born! Riders contemplate the large Mount Rundle limestone hotel in 1930. (CP)

On the terrace, guests admire the breathtaking scenery. (CP)

When they arrived at the "château", visitors were immediately captivated by the breathtaking view, the beautiful architecture, the grandeur of the decor and all the minute details that spell enchantment.

> The large brown limestone structure appears homogeneous despite its different building periods. The design is a Scottish Baronial derivation of the château style. There are no typical French medieval features at all — not even the familiar pointed dormers but rather those of the flat type — all arches are circular. Painter's central portion has round-headed windows, and the north wing has a Renaissance arcade before the large first floor lounge. This deviation from the château style is permissible because of the desired connections with Scotland, and since the CPR had no 'need' to recreate a French château.
>
> (Kalman, 1968)

The reference to the château style is a direct allusion to the style of Quebec City's Château Frontenac, to which a monumental centre tower had been added in 1924, just before the building of the "new" Banff Springs. The inspiration for the Château Frontenac, designed by the same architects who influenced the building of the Banff Springs (Bruce Price in 1892, Painter in 1910 and Edward and William Maxwell in 1924), was definitely that

The château-like structure, topped with steep copper roofs punctuated with turrets, finials, dormers and oriels. (Photo: Mark Anthony Price, 1996)

The large ornamented stained glass windows of Mount Stephen Hall enhance the beauty of the architecture of the courtyard. (Photo: Mark Anthony Price, 1996)

of a Loire Valley French château. Its asymmetrical design was marked by towers, dormers, steep copper roofs and walls of Scottish brick lightened by the rich gray Lachevrotière stone of its foundation walls, turrets and cornices.

Although one of the CPR's château-style hotels, the Banff Springs was very different from the Château Frontenac: it was very symmetrical, with a high centre tower flanked by two wings ending in smaller towers.

The Banff Springs was an exciting place to visit. What a thrill it was to sweep into the great stone courtyard and look through enchanted portals into the great baronial hall decorated with 16th century armour and buffalo heads. In keeping with the feudal atmosphere, a series of spacious halls featured stone floors and terraces, carved furniture, ancient armor, Medici prints, Leonardo tapestries and wrought iron. A stroll through the halls was and still is like embarking on a museum tour.

Balconies add an ornamental touch to the structure. One can see the quality of the workmanship. (Photo: Mark Anthony Price, 1996)

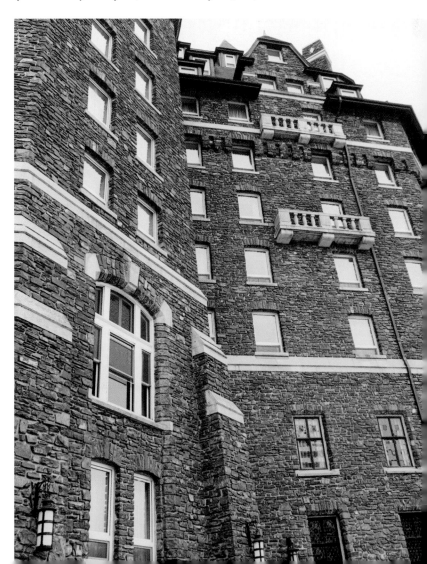

*Pamphlet watercolour by R.H. Palenske.
The CPR asked Canadian artists to produce
art to be used for advertising literature
for Europe and the United States.
Palenske, born in Woodstock Illinois, had an
advertising agency that had CP contracts.
He was also president of the Trail Riders
in 1935. He died in 1955. (CP)*

*The lobby has changed over the years
but is still reminiscent of a baronial hall.
This photograph was taken in the 1990's.
(CPH)*

The Mount Stephen Hall Wing

The Great Hall gives onto two of the most impressive spaces in the hotel, Mount Stephen Hall on one side and the Riverview Lounge (on the second floor) on the opposite side, in the north wing. Mount Stephen Hall occupies two stories. Its chief features include magnificent stained glass windows decorated with crests and coats of arms. It is furnished with rare antiques and old-world monastery reproductions. A balcony over the hall runs the length of the room, and inglenooks and cozy corners throughout add to the medieval atmosphere.

In the cloister walk, one cannot help but admire the decors chosen especially to emphasize the baronial atmosphere: five special Medici prints; *Sophie Arnold* by Grouse, in the Wallace Collection; *Madame Sophie de France* by Nattier; Gainsborough's *Dupont*; Viger-Lebrun's *Marie Antoinette* from Versailles National Museum; and Velasquez' *Infanta*

The vaulted Mount Stephen Hall named after the first president of the Canadian Pacific is still the most spectacular room in the hotel. (CPH)

Maria Teresa. The beauty of this plush gallery is enhanced by a collection of oriental rugs. It is but one of the many rooms that were designed with a profusion of prints for the wealthy European and American guests. The idea was to reproduce for the clients the atmosphere of their own private homes on the Continent.

It was said that Mount Stephen Hall, as shown in these two pictures from the 1930's, was like nothing else on this continent. It was furnished in rare antiques and reproductions from old world monasteries. (CP)

Detail of Mount Stephen Hall.
Crests adorn the stained glass windows.
(Photo: Mark Anthony Price, 1996)

Close-up of the carved oak ceiling
beams featuring the provincial crests.
(Photo: Mark Anthony Price, 1996)

Photograph of some of the stone work. Note the year of construction, 1928.
(Photo: Mark Anthony Price, 1996)

In the public rooms, great care was taken with the interior design. In addition to the collection of Medici prints in the Mount Stephen Gallery, one could admire nine House of Lords prints in the River-view Lounge, among which one finds *King John Signing the Magna Charta, 1215, Norman Phoenicians Trading with Ancient Britons* by Lord Leighten and the E. Crofts painting *Queen Elizabeth Visits the First Royal Exchange*.

The writing desk corner
in Mount Stephen Hall.
(Photo: Mark Anthony Price, 1996)

"...Such a gorgious view that I cannot
keep my eyes on the paper..." wrote a
prominent lady. R. H. Palenske surely
agreed. (CP)

Each room in the public section has reproductions of famous paintings, famous furniture
and famous stained glass. All in all, 21 crests
and mottos are to be found with the names of
the Canadian Pacific officials for whom they
were placed. These *objets d'art* throughout the
hotel give it a definite baronial flavour.

Representative of 15th century Gothic architecture, Mount Stephen Hall is one of
Canada's most renowned rooms. Grilled balcony, cloister walk, beamed ceiling and masonry lend the dignity of age. The floor is of irreg-
ular Bedford lime flagstone. Named for Lord
Mount Stephen, first president of the Canadian Pacific, this 'Great Hall' bears the arms of
the Dominion of Canada on one wall. Crests
of four presidents of the Canadian Pacific
Railway are worked in leaded glass windows.
The carved ceiling beams are buttressed by
crests of the provinces of New Brunswick,
Quebec, Manitoba, Prince Edward Island,
Ontario, Saskatchewan, Nova Scotia, Alberta
and British Columbia (NewFoundland was not
part of the confederation at the time). On one
wall is the insignia of the Royal Canadian
Mounted Police, official guardians of the
National Parks of Canada.

(Lazlo Funtek, CPR Archives)

The stained glass in the French
windows in Mount Stephen Hall
featured the crests and coats of
arms of presidents of the
Canadian Pacific Railway. (CP)

Detail of a cozy corner
of Spanish Walkway.
(Photo: Mark Anthony Price, 1996)

The baronial atmosphere is still very evident
in the Spanish Walkway. (CPH)

Decidedly Gothic, the Oak Room has kept all its charm. (CPH)

Dark wainscotting, antique furniture and soft lighting added romantic overtones to the atmosphere of the Oak Room in the 1930's. (CP)

Private dining rooms were hidden along the passageways off the foyer as shown in the 1930's and now. (CPH)

Next to the delightfully wainscoted and tapestried Oak Room, a spectacular recessed spiral staircase leads to the foyer above and two private dining rooms, the "Angus" and the "Strathcona" (named after R. B. Angus and Lord Strathcona), decorated in Norman Gothic style. From the foyer, guests go through magnificent bronze gates to enter the Alhambra dining room. This room, of Spanish Renaissance influence, is counterbalanced by the Cascade ballroom in the north wing. The proportions of the rooms in both wings, the elaborate ceilings and candelabras, the wainscoting and Persian rugs all enhance the impression of richness and the plush elegance and mystery that prevails everywhere.

Carved crown detail of the curved staircase.
Note the original tiffany lamp. (Photo: Mark Anthony Price, 1996)

Fossils are apparent in the Tyndall stone in the curved
staircase ascending from the end of Mount Stephen Hall
to the foyer of the Alhambra dining room. (Private collection)

The Alhambra foyer in 1930. Spanish influence
predominates in the decor. (CP)

Detail of the bronze doors. (Photo: Mark Anthony Price, 1996)

The bronze doors to the Alhambra dining room have been appraised at $30,000. (CP)

Watercolour by R.H. Palenske of the Alhambra dining room. A thousand people could dine at one time. (CP)

The furniture for these rooms was made by the Montreal company Castle and Son Manufacturing and consisted of exact replicas of original period pieces from European castles and manor houses. The rooms are very reminiscent of the opulent decor of the Château Frontenac in Quebec City, which had just been completed (in 1924) by Edward and William Maxwell and decorated under the tutelage of Mrs. Kate Reed. It is interesting to note that Mrs. Reed became the *grande dame* of decoration for the famous Canadian Pacific châteaux. This is borne out by all the CPR hotel ledgers and files which show, among other things, that all the furnishings came from Castle and Son in Montreal.

Mrs. Reed had died a few years earlier but her influence was still very strong. The tapestries, prints, rugs and furniture for the Banff Springs were selected by Michael Delahauty, a former manager of the hotel, and Kate Treleaven, personal secretary to CPR president Sir Edward Beatty. Kate Treleaven was also in charge of decoration and furnishings for the new Royal York Hotel in Toronto which opened in 1929.

The Riverview Lounge Wing

Continuing with our tour of Banff's "castle", after the Great Hall comes the north wing with its halls and suite which mirror those found in the south wing. The garden lounge became the Rob Roy dining room as we will see later. It extends the full length of the north wing. A large spiral staircase takes you up to the Riverview Lounge with its medieval decor: terrazzo floors, plaster walls with delicately molded columns crowned by elaborate capitals. The vaulted ceiling confirms the desire of the architect to toy with the medieval. The Fairholme dining room now called the Alberta Room is only divided from the Riverview Lounge by glazed arched openings in modern Renaissance style. In the lounge, eight immense arched windows brought from across the continent offer breathtaking views of the magnificent scenery of the Bow Valley and surrounding mountains. These windows are recessed so as to provide comfortable inglenooks.

The Riverview Lounge also boasts a fireplace with carved rams' heads of Tyndall stone and the prints *Portrait of a Young Man* by Giorgione and *Portrait of a Man* by Martin Burer as well as a reproduction of the famous Titian in the Frick Collection in New York: *Portrait of a Man*.

The Riverview Lounge, as shown here in the 1940's, on the upper level and the garden lounge on the lower level extended the full length of the north wing. (CP)

Two watercolours by R.H. Palenske of the Riverview Lounge in a pamphlet: the "million dollar view". (CP)

The Riverview Lounge fireplace with its carved rams' heads of Tyndall stone. (Photo: Mark Anthony Price, 1996)

The anteroom and staircase at the north end of the Riverview Lounge. At the far end the door of the library room, still in use in the 1940's but now closed. (CP)

Taken from the anteroom, this picture shows part of the oval room and lounge staircase, a copy of the Château Frontenac's circular staircase designed in 1892 by Bruce Price. (Photo: Mark Anthony Price, 1996)

The oval room in the1930's with its refined furniture. The oval room leads to the ballroom and the conservatory. (CPH)

Gracing the end of this wing is the Cascade ballroom, with a rich ceiling treated with carved beams and moulded and ornamented panels. The entire room was painted in very soft tones of gold and green with muted lighting provided by elaborate chandeliers. The romantic atmosphere carries over into the adjacent conservatory decorated at the time with a fountain of dark green marble.

The Cascade ballroom in the 1930's as presented by R. H. Palenske. (CP)

Detail of the Cascade ballroom with its rich ceiling treated with carved beams and moulded and ornamented panels. (Photo: Mark Anthony Price, 1996)

*The elegant conservatory, with its tile floors, palm trees and fountain,
was a favourite haunt of romantics. In 1928, the conservatory was the only area
still furnished with Kate Reed original furniture. (CPH)*

The conservatory as we can see it today with
the changes made to meet the needs of the hotel
and the guests. (Photo: Mark Anthony Price, 1996)

Watercolour by R. H. Palenske
of the conservatory
for a pamphlet. (CP)

The vice-regal suite has a medieval flair to it, with its vaulted ceilings and antique oak furniture. The natural light emanating from an antique curved glass fixture also creates a very special effect.(Photo: Mark Anthony Price, 1996)

A typical guest room from the 1930's. (CP)

Two 1940's suites. (CP)

In 1928, the new Banff Springs had 32 spectacular suites for its guests, including the Italian, Georgian, Tudor, Jacobean, Swiss, Empire, Art Déco and also one suite labeled "modernistic". The luxurious vice-regal suite had a decidedly medieval air about it, enhanced by vaulted ceilings, antique oak furniture, reproductions of old paintings and a remarkable collection of Persian rugs. It occupied the south wing tower and boasts three sitting rooms, one dining room and ten bedrooms.

As one meanders through the corridors and wings of the hotel one discovers other extraordinary rooms such as the library, a delightful little room of the Tudor period, or the writing room with its wonderful Persian rugs and paneled walls (complete with a real secret panel!) enlivened with prints of Scottish scenes.

Although there were no souvenir or sportswear shops anywhere in the hotel in 1928, a Curio Hall next to the Riverview Lounge offered English china, silver and souvenirs. As the guests stepped outside the lounge, they found themselves on large terraces overlooking the Bow valley, the garden terrace and the swimming pool terraces. They could feast their eyes on vistas of amazing grandeur, snow-capped mountain peaks towering in the blue sky, rushing ice green rivers and the dense unspoiled forests of Banff National Park.

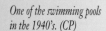

*One of the swimming pools
in the 1940's. (CP)*

*No matter which way
one looks, the scenery
is magnificent.
This is the hotel entrance
in the 1930's. (CP)*

*The Bow River Valley and
the Fairholme Range are a
fitting setting for this
hotel. The semi-circular
pool designed by Painter
overlooked a breathtaking
panorama. (CP)*

Ladies in haute couture creations prepare to enter the ballroom. Palenske watercolour. (CP)

From the beginning guests enjoyed dancing in the hotel's large rooms. Here they are dancing in the Cascade ballroom to the sound of the 1940's Banff Springs orchestra. (CP)

Those Were the Days!

Right from the beginning, the Banff Springs catered to an international clientele: wealthy, spoiled, ageless and very active! Life in the "castle" was for the privileged few. As one guest wrote: "one who stays here for two hours realizes the distinction between 'the man who lived in the terraced house and the brother in the streets below'… for one either stops at *The Hotel*, or he does not…".

The Canadian Pacific Railway promoted the Rockies not merely as pleasant scenery to be enjoyed but as a holiday destination with the Banff Springs as the focal point. The brilliant social life at Banff Springs was nothing if not highbrow! Night after night, against a backdrop of live musical entertainment and sparkling rainbow-tinted lights, beautiful, privileged women in fashionable gowns rubbed shoulders with distinguished gentlemen with the stamp of foreign courts upon them. It was a dazzling cosmopolitan crowd.

Louis Trono played at the Banff Springs for so many years that he was considered a living legend. (Louis Trono's personal collection)

Taking in the awe-inspiring scenery in the 1940's. (CP)

For the young and energetic guests of the Banff Springs, the day would start with a delicious breakfast served in their suite in view of the panorama of the Bow River and the mountains which beckoned to them. Looking through all the CPR pamphlets, they would realize what their dilemma was: too many things to do! Early mornings could be spent playing golf on the Stanley Thompson course with elk as their audience, or horseback riding or hiking. One of the advertising pamphlets waxed poetic about the "sea of peaks rippling away into tinted infinity" and the "exhilarating glacier-cooled atmosphere that is wine to the spirits and tireless energy to the body." It also extolled the virtues of demanding alpine climbs such as Mount Assiniboine as well as easier ascents which could be undertaken without the assistance of Swiss mountain guides.

Horseback riding in the mountains, a popular activity then and now. (CP)

The author trekking at Banff in the 1950's.
(Private collection)

Trail hikers near Banff in the 1940's. (CP)

The chiefs arriving in the great courtyard of the Banff Springs. (CP)

Noontime would often find our guests relaxing in the hot sulphur pool on the hotel's terrace and enjoying a refreshing drink. Luncheon was served fairly early as the afternoon was reserved for tennis. If they had timed their visit for a certain part of July, at the end of the afternoon there was a real surprise in store for these energetic guests: from different points all around the golf course members of the colourful Stoney tribe from the Morley Reserve would arrive in long files for a pow-wow. They were followed by people from the Sarcee, Blackfoot, Peigen and Cree bands. Resplendent in beadwork, ermine tails and eagle feathers they would ride up to the hotel courtyard. They paraded for the enjoyment of the guests in warrior and family groups and then settled down in their tents in the elk pasture near Buffalo Park. Tribal sports, bow and arrow contests, pony races, teepee-pitching contests, wrestling and horseback

Resplendent in their eagle feathers, ermine tails and beadwork costumes, the tribal members then settled down in their tents near Buffalo Park. (CP)

riding events were staged as the "Indian Days" started their three-day celebrations in July. It was the outfitter Tom Wilson, a legendary figure in Banff, who had initiated this show in 1889 to entertain the guests during the great rains that had washed out the CPR bridges.

Leaving the tents but hoping to return for the evening celebrations, guests would enjoy a welcome nap in their Jacobean or Tudor suite. Then it would be time to dress for dinner, the men in tuxedos and the ladies in elegant *haute couture* creations. There would be dancing in the ballroom all aglow in greens and gold under heavy chandeliers to the strains of quality music, provided by the Toronto Trio for example (with Murray Adaskin, Louis Crerar and Cornelius Ysselstyn), and the occasional glass of champagne by the fountain in the conservatory. After the dance some of our young guests would head for the billiards room and cigars while others enjoyed the moonlight dances of the Stoneys as they sang songs taught to them by their elders. A slow walk back under the moon, with the turrets and pinnacles of the grand hotel silhouetted against the high peaks. One had to be torn away from such an awesome sight!

Native peoples at Banff in an official poster. The original painting hangs in the entrance of the golf clubhouse. (CP)

Famous painting depicting what would be an unusual sight today. (CP)

The Highland Gathering, a Scottish music, sports and dancing festival, were very popular with hotel guests. Palenske pamphlet watercolour. (CP)

The Highland Gathering was inaugurated in 1927. (CP)

The CPR was always devising new forms of entertainment for the pleasure of their guests. And what entertainment it was! The "Indian Days" celebration was one of the most colourful spectacles on the North American continent. Another popular event created for the guests was the Highland Gathering inaugurated in 1927. This was a Scottish festival of music and sports, complete with bagpipers from highland regiments brought in to play and dance.

CPR poster promoting the coast-to-coast crossing of Canada by train. Harry Hudson Rodmell, 1921. (CP)

R.H. Palenske. (CP)

To help attract people to its hotels at Banff and Lake Louise, the CPR readily agreed to sponsor the Trail Riders of the Canadian Rockies (and later their sister organizations the Skyline Hikers and the Ski Runners) and to advertize world-wide. Every year, a four-day Official Ride was held starting at Lake Windermere, Banff or Lake Louise. A note of interest: the reservations for this event were made in advance not at Banff but at Windsor Station in Montreal.

Anyone for Golf?

Another one of the Banff Springs Hotel's big attractions was its golf course. The first course was built in 1911. This 9-hole course was taken over by the government between 1917 and 1927 because the Canadian Pacific had wanted to raise the rates. In 1927 The CP got the course back and had Stanley Thompson rebuild it. It set a precedent as the most expensive golf course in the world.

> An 18 hole golf course, superbly located on the banks of the Bow River and guarded by huge bastions of rock, turreted and pinnacled like the fortified castle of old, has been entirely reconstructed under supervision of Stanley Thompson and offers one of the most scenically beautiful courses in the world. It is said to have a length of 6,640 yards and a par of 73.
>
> (CPR pamphlet, 1928)

In 1928, *Construction* magazine announced the building of the golf course in these words:

> Canada will shortly possess one of the nicest and most beautiful golf courses in the world at Banff. Assisted by an army of skilled workmen Stanley Thompson of Toronto, internationally known golf architect, has made rapid progress with the construction of the new championship golf course and present indications are that the course will take its place at the top of the list of golf links on this continent, whether inland or seaside.

The first golf clubhouse at the Banff Springs.

Located as it was on the "roof of the world" and surrounded by the most magnificent mountain scenery imaginable, the Banff Springs course was unique. It was of full championship length, with the plans calling for a yardage of 6,690. There were also two other sets of tees with a respective yardage of 6,315 and 6,095. These tees were covered in grass and were in use the whole time. The bunkering had been so carefully worked out that each set of tees practically amounted to a different course. The fairways too were double width and there were two distinct routes to each hole.

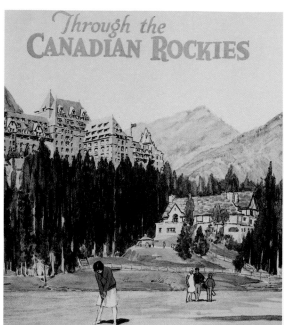

Through the
CANADIAN ROCKIES

*A new golf clubhouse
later replaced this smaller
structure. It now houses
the Waldhaus restaurant.
(CP)*

*Stanley Thompson designed
one of the most beautiful
courses in the world for the
Banff Springs.*

*The ten years leading up to
World War II were really the golden years
for the Banff Springs Hotel. (CP)*

Stanley Thompson

Stanley Thompson was born in Toronto in 1894. He was one of five brothers who dominated Canadian golf like no family since: Frank won the Canadian Amateur championship in 1921 and 1924; William won in 1923; Matt and Nicol were professional for 50 years and Stanley won medal honours at the 1922-1923 Canadian Amateur championships.

But it was as a designer of Canada's finest courses that Stanley achieved greatness. "Thompson", wrote his biographer Tim O'Connor, "was a master of strategic design and routing, a creative free thinker who often used principles of art in transforming dirt and bushes into golf holes — that's one reason his West courses are captivating in ways that escape most golfers".

The Canadian Pacific Railway hired him to design a course near Banff at a cost of one million dollars. That made the course the most expensive ever built when it was opened in 1928. In all, Thompson designed more than 125 golf courses, most of them in Canada. Although his work included the US, the Caribbean and South America, he won international acclaim for Jasper and Banff which are regarded as two of the world's best mountain courses.

The ten years leading up to World War II were really the golden years for the Banff Springs Hotel and the CP Railway. Banff and Lake Louise, the two "jewels" in the western hotel collection, were described as "exotic playgrounds on top of this world". Furthermore, the exquisite drawings and paintings of the best artists of the day, photographs, pamphlets and fabulous posters were luring tourists to undertake the trip from Liverpool to Singapore on the company's White Star ships and in the elegant trains crossing Canada from Halifax to Vancouver with the inescapable stop in the Rockies.

(CP)

The Second Era of a Grand Hotel

1930 to 1987

By 1930, the Canadian Pacific's operations had grown and, with its cruise steamship lines, railway lines and grand new hotels, its tourist facilities extended from Liverpool to Hong Kong.

Two new railway lines were fiercely competing for clients: the Canadian Northern and the Grand Trunk Pacific which were combined and nationalized in 1919 to form the Canadian National Railways. This government company was provided with ample subsidies to establish a new rail empire, especially in the west. Following Van Horne's successes and borrowing all his marketing ideas, the Canadian National operated the Jasper Park Lodge and created a series of mountain activities similar to those in the Banff/Lake Louise area.

The glorious days of the grand hotel in the Rockies came to a halt with the Depression and World War II. The terrible depression combined with lost revenues during World War II devastated Canadian Pacific Hotel properties in the Rockies. A nearly fatal blow to the properties followed after the war when visitor travel patterns changed. As aircraft became economical to build and reliable and safe to use, they replaced trains and steamships as the most popular means of long distance travel. Prosperity and the perfection of the automobile changed the way people travelled

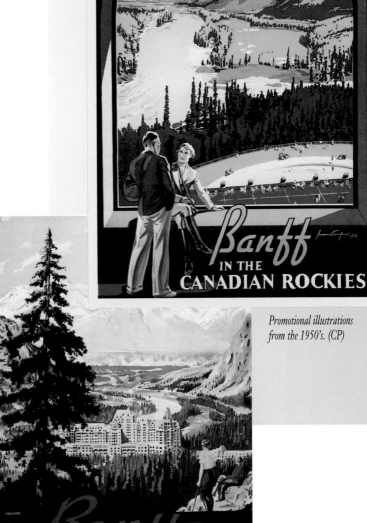

Promotional illustrations from the 1950's. (CP)

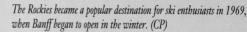

trains and lure them across Canada and out west. But in the fifties and the sixties the Canadian Pacific Company was more interested in new financial ventures than in its numerous hotels. The Banff Springs grew hopelessly out-of-date in comparison with the new Hiltons and other attractive, modern hotels.

By the mid-1960's, the grand railway hotels in the Rockies were run down and overwhelmingly expensive to maintain. An offer to purchase the Canadian Pacific Hotel chain was made by a major international hotel consortium. This offer, however, was made with the condition that the buyer did not have to take CP's money-losing Banff National Park properties. There was talk of tearing down the Banff Springs and the Chateau Lake Louise. Canadian Pacific Hotels did not want to abandon its historical place in the western mountain parks, though. An enormous amount of work would have to be done to save them, and this could only be done at great sacrifice by those who believed the hotels could be revived.

If the great CPR hotels in the Banff National Park were to survive these difficult times, new programs were needed. Finally, in 1969, it was decided that Banff Springs would be kept open during the winter, with skiers as the main target clientele. This was a major move and one that proved to be a remarkably successful one. The CPR embarked on a vast advertising campaign to attract clients to the hotels in winter. In 1969, the magazine *Ski Life* printed this appreciation of the Banff Springs' ski programs:

and what they wanted to see. New destinations sprang up all over North America, and some of the old ones fell into decline.

The elegance, the display of wealth, the extravagance of European-style tourism were never to return. After the war, business deteriorated. For twenty-five years, the CPR had staged ambitious marketing and promotion campaigns to entice tourists onto its great

Until recently the skiers would head for Europe — But thanks to the efforts of the Banff, Lake Louise and Jasper associates Canadians are now recognizing their own paradise: a western wilderness of incomparable beauty which offers skiing that can match with anything anywhere... The names Banff, Lake Louise and Jasper will soon be on tongue tips throughout the skiing world.

(CPR Archives)

In 1969, lvor Petrak arrived and became general manager in charge of the Banff Springs and Château Lake Louise.

It became his mission to bring the Banff Springs back to life and give its image a boost. He attacked the problems of revamping it with fierce determination. The whole building was crumbling; plaster, paint, flooring, furniture, appliances, heating — everything was in total disarray. Petrak engaged in a battle to renew the old hotel to its former glory, a battle that would last up to his retirement in 1991.

His message to his staff was clear: "People who come here are dreamers and they want to live in a real castle... So we don't sell rooms, we sell a dream." Petrak felt strongly about the need for management to build the best relations possible with the staff and everybody who worked around and in the castle. He considered this his best accomplishment.

Winter publicity for the Banff Springs Hotel. (CP)

The beauty of the winter scenery. View from one of the hotel rooms facing the Fairlhome River. (Photo: France Gagnon Pratte)

Our West is best. (CP)

Petrak believed that the hotel could become the centre of a much expanded winter season in Banff which he hoped to develop. The plan to open the Banff Springs for the first time in the winter of 1969 had been a costly one. Like the Chateau Lake Louise, the Springs was not properly insulated for winter operation. A great deal of engineering was required to guarantee a steady supply of heat to the rooms and to ensure that the electricity stayed on in every part of the hotel.

Petrak knew that a regular income would be necessary to pay for the high costs of winter operations and still allow the hotel to make the continuous improvements required to restore the property to its former grandeur. To ensure these revenues he had to cultivate the winter ski market. Even with a room rate of only $14.00 a night, there were often only a dozen people in the hotel during the early part of the winter. By February of 1972, Petrak had the whole hotel open and full. Later, Petrak hired a star on the French national ski team named Audrey de Baghy to help draw the international ski market.

Petrak then expanded the successful package concept into the spring season. Next were incentive tours to strengthen business in both spring and fall. The oil crises of 1973 meant that Petrak had to rethink the hotel's entire sales strategy Busses suddenly became a serious

Ivor Petrak

Born in Czechoslovakia in 1922, Ivor Petrak first studied law in Prague. After graduating he worked in some of the best hotels and resorts in Europe. In the summer of 1950 he was invited to join Sheraton Hotels in Canada. While in Toronto in 1951 Petrak was asked to work with Canadian Pacific Hotels as head waiter at Chateau Lake Louise. He then went to Stowe in Vermont where he stayed for 10 years. It is at Stowe that he mastered the art of personal service and learned to maximize the use of hotel space with careful renovation. While in Vermont, he was once again asked by Canadian Pacific Hotels to come to the Banff Springs hotel.

Ivor Petrak and designer Lazlo Funtek in the modern presidential suite. (CPH)

alternative to cars. The Banff Springs would cater to tours during the busy summer months. By 1974, the hotel had 100% occupancy from June through September. The success of the Banff Springs was changing the town and its place in Canadian tourism. But Petrak was not done. There was one market that hadn't even been tapped. While having lunch at a restaurant in Frankfurt, Germany in October of 1972, Petrak watched for two hours as a steady line of Japanese visitors passed in single file by his table. He couldn't wait to get home. A good man was put in charge of carrying out Petrak's wishes, Jean Cimon.

Petrak and Cimon concocted ski packages in the "wild Rockies" that proved to be irresistible. The rotund Cimon was a genius at promoting the Banff Springs as the best place in the world to be. He even went so far as to dance in Scottish attire (kilt and bagpipes no less) and managed to get himself invited to appear on Japan's most popular talk show with

Kai Ohashi, the Johnny Carson of the East. Thousands of Japanese followed Cimon to the Rockies to stay at its grand hotels.

So that he would be prepared for his Japanese and other guests, Petrak went ahead with his plans to refurbish the entire hotel. Starting with 75 rooms the first year and continuing with 150 rooms per year after that, Petrak renovated the building. He asked consultant designer Lazlo Funtek from the Banff Centre for the Arts to take care of the new decor. Soon a new dining room offered an unparalleled view of the entire Bow Valley.

Borrowed furniture from other CP hotels graced the rooms and halls of the hotel at Banff. This is the Riverview Lounge in the 1970's. (CP)

An accent of the 70's: the white panels on top of the upper section of the main lobby. (CP)

*The Garden Lounge,
in 1969; this large room
became the Rob Roy Dining
Room under Petrak's
management. (CP)*

*The Rob Roy Dining Room,
one of the most delightful
dining rooms in Banff. (Photo:
Mark Anthony Price, 1996)*

Detail of the furniture of the Rob Roy Dining Room, replicas of pieces from European castles. (Photo: Mark Anthony Price, 1996)

Called the Rob Roy Dining Room, it filled the space formerly occupied by the Garden Lounge. The large circular swimming pool on the terrace was rebuilt for summer and winter, and served as a steaming bath for sports enthusiasts. Unfortunately, though, the beautifully designed semi-circular pool was later replaced by a small rectangular one.

Business was definitely booming, so new spaces needed to be created. Petrak and Funtek decided to enclose all the hotel's outside terraces in glass, thus creating a coffee room at the end of the lobby, a large Van Horne Room, an Admiralty Suite and many additional public rooms. The innovative glass-enclosed terraces were detrimental to the exterior design of the Banff Springs, however, and reduced the visual impact of the great stone walls of the baronial castle. They countered the desired austerity of the stone walls and reduced the overall effect sought by architect William Painter.

The modern glassed-in terrace overlooking the courtyard. (Photo: Mark Anthony Price, 1996)

However, the numerous glass additions were not so permanent as to be irreversible.

Ivor Petrak had succeeded in turning the hotel around as promised. He had brought it up to date.

The glass-enclosed terrace named after Ivor Petrak provided extra space for Petrak's skiing and convention clientele. (Photo: Mark Anthony Price, 1996)

During Ivor Petrak's time, two staircases were added to the south wing to serve as fire escapes. (Photo: Mark Anthony Price, 1996)

Ivor Petrak in front of the Banff Springs. (CPH)

The Grapes Wine Bar is one of the many food and beverage rooms that have been added to the hotel since the 1970's. (CP)

Petrak's vision called for every room and every corner of the hotel to be rented and occupied and, in his enthusiasm, he was known to overbook. Some guests had to be put up in odd places such as the Oak Room! He badly needed to attract new visitors in order to pay for new facilities and rooms. When he was unable to get any funds from the CPR board, he even borrowed unused furniture from various hotels such as the Royal York in Toronto to upgrade the public rooms.

The Tudor House had been home to the staff since the beginning. Petrak decided to turn this building into a guest wing, named the Manor Wing, which was connected by a passageway to the new conference centre. Having converted the 245-room staff house into this guest wing, accommodations needed to be found for the staff. Numerous staff houses and apartments were built on the West side of Spray avenue which blended well with the surrounding mountains. Petrak then created spaces everywhere for more clients and started up the convention business in the hotel. By 1988, the Banff Springs could accommodate 1,750 guests at one time. There were 828 bedrooms in the hotel and 13 meeting rooms that are converted into bedrooms in summer. Many of the rooms could be linked together to form the hotel's 66 suites.

Throughout this tremendous task of resurrecting a decaying hotel so it would be on a par with the great resorts of North America, Petrak had a new ally: William Stinson, who became president of the Canadian Pacific in 1981 and was elected chief executive officer in 1985. Stinson was deeply inspired by Van Horne's vision for the railway company and that vision included the remaking and revival of all the CPR's palatial hotels.

The Samuraï Japanese restaurant is one of the hotel's more recently restored dining room facilities. (CPH)

Carved crest on the upper part of the bar entrance. (Photo: Mark Anthony Price, 1996)

The Grapes Wine Bar, formerly the Writing Room, is warm and intimate with its dark wood walls. (Photo: Mark Anthony Price, 1996)

This rectangular outdoor pool replaced the spectacular semi-circular pool designed by Walter Painter. In winter the saltwater pool becomes a "hot tub". (CPH)

President William Stinson made the decision to upgrade the great château-like railway hotels: the Banff Springs, Château Lake Louise, the Empress, the Palliser and eventually all the others. It took a vision, an indomitable will and the securing of adequate funding to the tune of millions of dollars. A new company was formed — Canadian Pacific Hotels and Resorts — with Robert DeMone as President.

In his efforts to make Canadian Pacific's mountain hotels the finest resorts in the world, Ivor Petrak liked to think that he was fulfilling the ambitions of nineteenth century railway visionary William Cornelius Van Horne. Keeping these famous heritage hotels in operation was one of Petrak's greatest achievments. Ivor Petrak retired from Canadian Pacific Hotels in 1991, and was succeeded by Edward Kissane.

Under Ted Kissane, the Banff Springs Hotel was finally restored to its former grandeur. (CP)

Rebirth of a Château
The 1990's

Mount Stephen Hall, clothed in its enchanting Christmas decorations. (CPH)

More years of intense work were again needed to bring the hotel up to European standards. The new manager Edward Kissane had the ability to understand the spirit of the place as well as the energy and the determination and the commitment it would take to complete the restoration.

Ted Kissane wanted to enhance the atmosphere of his château. Commenting on the passage of time and the hotel he confided: "The hotel needs to attract the best of the European and worldly clientele to the best of facilities." It is the incredible atmosphere that prevails within the stately walls that makes the hotel what it is. The vaulted ceilings, the stone walls, the impressive staircases, the antique furniture and the decor throughout have been there for over a hundred years. Restoring the elegance and simplicity of the original interiors has proven to be extremely successful in attracting people from around the world.

When Kissane arrived in Banff in the spring of 1990, he was faced immediately with the challenge of compléting Canadian Pacific's rescue plan for the Banff Springs Hotel, Chateau Lake Louise and the recently acquired Jasper Park Lodge. With CP Chairman Bill Stinson's decision to commit approximately $100 million in new capital towards the restoration of the Banff Springs, it was now Kissane's mission to develop a plan to utilize those funds in a way that would recreate the grandeur of the Banff Springs Hotel as it was at the turn of the century. Not only would the hotel have to be completely restored,

Edward Kissane

Edward (Ted) Kissane was born in Rochester, New York in 1944. During his early childhood, his family moved to Vermont. Mr. Kissane's first exposure to resorts was during summers in high school and college. After a few summers working at a resort and having undertaken studies in Business Administration at Valley Forge Military Academy and Colorado State University, he decided to take a year off from school and work at the Arizona Biltmore in the Gold Room Restaurant. It was during this time that he realized a calling in the hotel industry and decided to pursue a degree in Hotel Management at Paul Smith's College in upstate New York. Upon graduation, Ted Kissane was chosen as a management trainee with the prestigious Sheraton Corporation.

At the age of only 26, he became Assistant to the General Manager at the Sheraton Park Hotel in Washington, DC and at the age of 29 became Resident Manager at the Sheraton Carlton in the same city. Over the next 20 years, Kissane developed a reputation for being able to build strong management teams and improve the operations of hotels to which he was assigned. He managed many Sheraton properties including opening the Sheraton Park Central Hotel in Dallas, Texas. He became a Regional Vice President with Sheraton at age 36.

In 1988, Kissane was lured away from Sheraton to become Senior Vice-President, Director of Operations for Beacon Hospitality Hotel Company in Boston. Ted felt there was one thing he still wanted to do in his career. He had still not had the opportunity to manage a great resort. In February 1990, Paul O'Neil, a well-known and highly-regarded hotel executive, called his former collegue to offer him the "best resort job in North America". Kissane was astonished to discover this hotel was the Banff Springs Hotel, run by Ivor Petrak for the past twenty years. When Ted visited Banff, the retiring Petrak encouraged him to take his job.

Both the sun room on the ground floor and the Rundle Room on the second floor of the central tower offer a magnificent view of the Rockies. They contribute to the hotel's elegance today. (CPH)

but the quality of guest services needed to be greatly enhanced to justify the investment.

Kissane's strategy was to develop a restoration program that was respectful of the hotel's heritage, and complement it with the finest staff training possible. Due to the seasonality of the hotel in the past, staff training was never a priority as the staff was comprised largely of students working summers. During the 1990's Kissane directed a great deal of the hotel's resources to improving guest services and employee relations. New and improved employee recruiting methods were implemented and training programs reduced employee turnover by more than two-thirds.

Kissane's management philosophy was simple. As far as he was concerned, the formula for success was to exceed the expectations of three groups. The first group was the shareholders of the parent company, Canadian Pacific Limited; the second group was made up of the hotel's employees; and the third group comprised of the hotel's guests. Every management decision needed to respect the needs and the values of each of these groups. The strategy has paid off as the hotel has once again become a successful enterprise and one of the best known hotels in the world.

Ted Kissane's plan of action was two-fold: first, to totally upgrade the Banff Springs Hotel and second, to introduce the renewed Banff Springs to the world. With the collaboration of architect Robert LeBlond and designer Kerry Busby of Calgary, Kissane initiated the huge undertaking of bringing back the elegance and simplicity of the original decors using contemporary methods and modern equipment.

For example, the Cascade ballroom and adjoining staircase have returned to their original soft colours and the conservatory — rediscovered after many years — recreates a colourful addition to the ballroom.

An arched passage connects the hotel to the conference centre.
It was built in 1988 and like the conference centre it blends in perfect
harmony with the 1928 hotel. Note the stonecutters' and masonry work.
(Mark Anthony Price, 1996)

The first accomplishment called for by the rejuvenation of the Banff Springs was the construction of the conference centre which opened in November 1990. Designed by Carruthers, Marshall and Associates and built at a cost of $25 million, the large structure is in perfect harmony with the grand hotel. The architects used two million pounds of Rundle rock to create a facade similar to that of the older buildings, topped with high roofs punctuated with gables and a fenestration similar to that of the hotel. Visually, the conference centre is perfectly integrated to the whole and adds to the complex without breaking the architectural harmony. The semi-circular centre has a large round courtyard with a garden

The conference centre was designed by Carruthers, Marshall and Associates from Calgary. In the courtyard stands the statue commemorating Sir William Cornelius Van Horne. (CPH)

The interior design was done by Kerry Busby and reflects in a more modern way the atmosphere of the hotel. (CPH)

The furnishings at the entrance of the Crump Room in the conference centre are in warm tones of gold and green. (CPH)

where one can admire William Cornelius Van Horne himself, cast in bronze and presiding again over the destinies of the CP.

Occupying 150,000 square feet at the foot of Mount Rundle and built to accommodate as many conventions as possible in any given year, the conference centre is equipped with 29 suites, a grand ballroom for 1,600 persons, a theatre with a seating capacity of 250 as well as meeting and conference rooms of all sizes. The principal elevation of the centre encloses a plaza for arriving guests and visitors. The reception rooms bear the names of past presidents Van Horne, Shaughnessy, Beatty, Crump and Coleman. The passageway leads to the Manor Wing, Pavilion Restaurant, Tudor House and, by way of a second skywalk, the main hotel lobby.

Solace

Solace Spa logo:
solus par aqua.
(CPH)

To revive the spa tradition that was so much a part of the "discovery" of the Rockies, Ted Kissane wanted to reinstate the Banff custom of "taking the waters". He asked architect Robert LeBlond of Calgary to design a spa in the best European tradition and incorporate it to the hotel. It is interesting to read the architect's own words regarding his vision of Solace, the Banff Springs Spa:

Architecture is based on more than just wood and stone in that it must dialogue with the users of the facilities we design and convey a sense of place, atmosphere or a feeling of belonging... It is only by seeking to create this centre of gravity, or heart and soul, of each and every project that we may be able to once in a while arrive at a solution that is head and shoulders above what has been done before. We have made that commitment to reach for the stars for our clients and to build dream projects for them. We create buildings that celebrate the process of living as opposed to being totally utilitarian in nature.

These remarks aptly describe the philosophy behind the concept and design for the $12-million spa complex.

The spa dreamed of by Ted Kissane and designed by Robert LeBlond enhances the medieval-like atmosphere of the hotel with its traditional attributes. LeBlond calls the design elegant without falling into ostentation. The interior epitomizes warmth and serenity. It is a celebration of the human body and its wellness in its relationship to the natural environment. It is a place for meditation and relaxation, a place where one can rediscover oneself (Paterson).

The European-style Solace Spa with its indoor and outdoor mineral pools opened in 1995: "retreat within a retreat". (CPH)

Kerry Busby, Ted Kissane and Robert LeBlond (CPH)

The tradition of "taking the waters" is a centuries-old ritual of rejuvenation. The Hungarian Kur treatment has been instituted at Solace. The Kur bath, world-renowned for its high content of mineral and trace elements, helps improve circulation and muscle and joint mobility while enhancing over-all health. Solace comes from the Latin phrase *solus par aqua* (SPA) meaning "health by water".

The new building recreates the feeling of the great halls and austere walls of the Banff Springs translated into a new space full of light, water and luxury. The Solace mineral pool is breathtakingly lovely with its tiles and mosaics in blues and greens and a large vaulted skylight that infuses the interior with rays of sunshine. The pool itself is equipped with an underwater speaker system. The spa is now one of the most picturesque features of Banff. The amazing creation of this totally new structure in complete accordance with the existing building is remarkable.

This 35,000 square foot spa is graced with three waterfalls and an equal number of fireplaces, private solariums and all the whirlpools, saunas and therapeutic treatment rooms one could wish for. In addition, there are private gyms and a private restaurant with terraces opening out onto outdoor whirlpools and swimming areas.

The design is such that it relates strongly to the existing hotel character but with an architectural vocabulary that speaks of honesty, integrity and simplicity. The structure belongs very clearly within its setting and is friendly and compatible with its immediate environment.

— Robert LeBlond

The renowned golf course with its 27 holes and new clubhouse designed by Robert LeBlond. (CPH)

But the spa was not the only new project by architect Robert LeBlond: he also designed a golf clubhouse to service an additional nine holes. Inspired by the teepee of the plains natives and built entirely of wood, the modern building is the signature of the new architectural concept chosen by LeBlond and blends with and enhances the surrounding mountain scenery. Golf professional Doug Wood reigns here over this realm of golfers, the ever present elk and the occasional grizzly.

The interior of the "teepee" clubhouse.
(Photo: Mark Anthony Price,1996)

Something for Everyone

The conference centre, the spa and the golf course addition had put the Banff Springs back on the map as far as international stature was concerned. An extensive renovation and public relations program was still needed, however, to restore public and private spaces to the same level of excellence and tell the world about the great hotel.

As the Banff Springs reached the final phase of its complete overhaul, the second component of Ted Kissane's plan kicked in: the "selling of the Banff Springs" campaign comparable to the publicity put together by the CPR at the beginning of the century. A new public relations and communications division was set up to take on this huge task and it has proven very successful. Now, four seasons

The staff choir singing during the hotel's month-long Christmas season. (CPH)

programs are created to entice pleasure-seekers, outdoor enthusiasts and just plain family types from around the world with fabulous events of all sorts. The International Wine and Food Festival is one such event and it alone brings 600 participants every year and has won acclaim as Canada's premier culinary extravaganza.

A special walking tour takes guests through the hotel's 107 years of existence as they explore enchanting hallways and great rooms. The best new event, however, is indisputably the Festival of Christmas, which lasts from mid-November to early January. This celebration includes musical entertainment and children's shows — complete with jugglers, buskers, strolling choirs and musicians. Every

Storytelling at Christmas.
(CPH)

Canadian Pacific interpretive guide Mike Vincent at the Abbot Hut above Lake Louise. (CPH)

night the hotel springs to life with the Christmas tree lighting ceremony as Santa, the Nutcracker and the Sugarplum Fairy lead a parade of colourful characters through the "castle" halls. A very humane feature was introduced by Ted Kissane himself: a storytelling hour before bedtime for all the children staying at the hotel. He participates in the storytelling personally and encourages staff members to donate one hour of their time every night to charm the children. Called the "Spirit of Christmas Past", this magical interlude in the stately sylvan retreat has proven irresistible for families, who flock to the Banff Springs at Christmas time!

The Banff Springs National Parks Heritage Commitment

It is especially fitting that the mountaineering tradition has regained its historical status in Ted Kissane's renewed vision for the Banff Springs. The re-creation of the Swiss guides mountaineering program features a number of very significant heritage experiences and learning opportunities.

In keeping with early 19th century mountaineering tradition, this program will introduce the Banff Springs' guests to the joys of trekking, the challenge of testing one's limits and, last but not least, the sheer pleasure of gazing at some of the most beautiful panoramas of the Rockies. With this endeavour, Ted Kissane will be adding a new and exciting dimension to holidaying at Banff and give guests a true sense of what the Banff National Park means to Canadians.

Renewed Partnership

The circumstances national parks face today are much different than those they encountered when the first great hotel helped knit the mountain parks into the beginning of a national system. The kinds of visitors national parks attract have changed and so have their demands. Since the hot springs were set aside in 1885, visitation to Canada's first national park has increased thousands of times. The sheer task of getting national parks messages out to all these visitors has become overwhelming.

As a national historic site in its own right and an important park attraction, the Banff Springs plays an active and vital role in the shaping of quality visitor experiences. Because of its famous reputation and because it hosts hundreds of thousands of park visitors every year, the Banff Springs Hotel has been a great asset to Banff National Park in encouraging further public understanding, appreciation and sustainable enjoyment of Canadian heritage landscapes.

ROBERT SANDFORD

AN INTERNATIONAL VISION FOR THE NEXT CENTURY

For over a hundred years, the destiny of the Banff Springs has been exceptional. Protected within the bounds of Banff National Park, which has been classified as a historical site by the Government of Canada, this stately, baronial castle in the heart of the Rockies has witnessed the passage of time with dignity and resilience.

The vision for the Banff Springs Hotel is one of a grand palatial hotel with an international clientele from all continents. In an atmosphere reminiscent of the glorious Van Horne days but blending with the most modern of facilities, guests will bask in exquisite surroundings.

The Banff Springs was created as a haven of peace in the midst of the wilderness, as an architectural gem and a place where you dream to return, and it has endured for over a hundred years. It is the vision of the people who presided over its destiny that has sustained the dream. So, as we enter the new millennium, it is most fitting to salute them with the appreciation and simple words of William Cornelius Van Horne: "The work has been well done in every way".

The Banff Springs Hotel.
(CP)

Archives

Banff Springs Hotel Archives, Banff

Canadian Pacific Railway Company Archives, Montréal

Cornell University Archives

McGill University Archives, Montréal

Whyte Museum of the Canadian Rockies Archives, Banff

Microfilm

Graybill, S. Sr, *Bruce Price, American Architect,* 1845 - 1903

On microfilm, Yale University 1957 - McGill University Archives

Periodicals

Caraffe, Marc de and Janet Wright. "Les hôtels de style château des compagnies ferroviaires." *Agenda Paper*, Historic Sites and Monuments Board of Canada, 1980

Ferree, Barr. "A Talk with Bruce Price." *The Architectural Record*, 1899

Newman, Peter. "Sir William Van Horne, The National Builder." *The Montrealer*, June 1959

Price, Bruce. "A Large Country House." *Modern Architectural Practice*, 1887

Rogatnik, Abraham. "Canadian Castles: The Phenomenon of the Railway Hotel." *Architectural Review*, 1967

Sturgis, Russell. "A Critique of the Architecture of Bruce Price." *The Architectural Record*, 1899

"Banff Springs." *Construction*, 1928

Books

Berton, Pierre. *The Last Spike.* Toronto: McClelland & Stewart, 1971

Berton, Pierre. *The National Dream.* Toronto: McClelland & Stewart, 1970

Choko, Marc H. and David L. Jones. *Canadian Pacific Posters 1883-1963.* Montréal: Meridian Press, 1988

Gagnon Pratte, France. *Country Houses for Montrealers: The Architecture of Edward and W.S. Maxwell, 1892-1924.* Montréal: Meridian Press, 1987

Gagnon Pratte, France and Éric Etter. *The Château Frontenac.* Québec: Continuité, 1993

Gibson, John Murray. *The Romantic History of the Canadian Pacific.* New York: Van Rees Press, 1935

Hart, E.J. *The Selling of Canada. The CPR and the Beginnings of Canadian Tourism.* Banff: Altitude Publishing, 1983

Kalman, Harold D. *The Railway Hotels and the Development of the Château Style in Canada.* Victoria, B.C: University of Victoria, 1968

Lamb, Kaye. *History of the Canadian Pacific.* New York: McMillan Pub. Co., 1977

Mayles, Stephen. *William Van Horne.* Don Mills: Fitzhenry & Whiteside, 1983

Parker, Patricia. *The Feather and the Drum, 1889 - 1972.* Calgary: Consolidated Communications, 1990

Pole, Graeme. *The Canadian Rockies.* Banff: Altitude Publishing, 1991

Robinson, Bart. Banff Springs: *The Story of a Hotel.* Banff: Summerthought, 1973

Sandford, Robert. *The Canadian Alps. The History of Mountaineering in Canada.* Banff: Altitude Publishing, 1991

Sandford, Robert and G. Powter. *Canadian Summits.* Canmore: The Alpine Club of Canada, 1994

Vaughan, Walter. *The Life and Work of Sir William Van Horne.* New York: The Century Company, 1920

Wilson, R.G. *Victorian Resorts and Hotels.* New Haven: Victorian Society of America, 1982

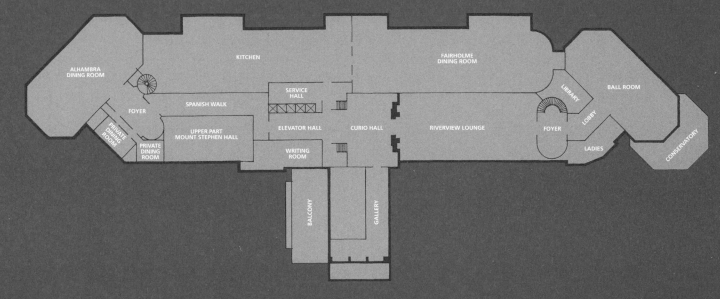

First floor, 1925

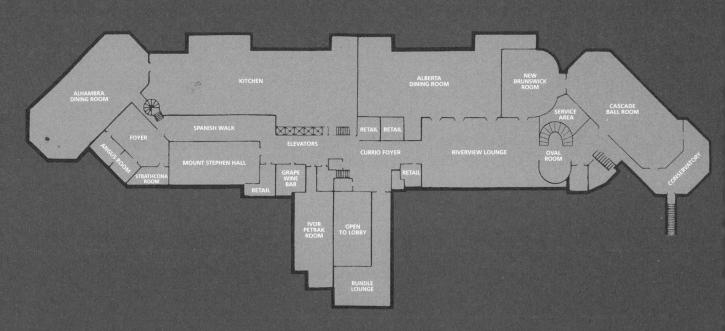

Mezzanine level, 1990